Amazing Trifle Reci

42 Easy To Prepare Layered Desserts

Previously titled "Delicious Trifle Recipes 2"

By

Dan Moyer

Photography By:

Brian Gohacki

Cover Design By:

John Patrick George

Table Of Contents

Notes From Family Of The Author 3

Introduction 4

Banana Cream Pie Trifle 6

Blackberry Crisp Trifle 7

Blueberry Pie Trifle 8

Brownie Ice Cream Sundae Trifle 9

Butterscotch Toffee Bar Trifle 10

Cherry Cheesecake Trifle 11

Cherry Lemon Trifle 12

Cherry Vanilla Trifle 13

Chocolate Chip Cookie Dough Trifle 14

Chocolate Covered Strawberry Trifle 15

Chocolate Lovers' Trifle 16

Chocolate Malt Ball Trifle 18

Chocolate Rum Cake Trifle 19

Cinnamon Apple Cheesecake Trifle 20

Cinnamon Donut Trifle 21

CMP Trifle 22

Coconut Cream Pie Trifle 23

Coffee Cake Trifle 24

Cookies N' Cream Cheesecake Trifle 25

English Trifle With Sherry 26

Fudge Trifle 28

Key Lime Pie Trifle 29

Lemon Blueberry Trifle 30

Macadamia Nut Cookie Trifle 31

Maple Cheesecake Trifle 32

Maple Pecan Trifle 33

Maple Pumpkin Trifle 34

Marshmallow Trifle 35

Mint Chocolate Chip Cheesecake Trifle 36

Mocha Walnut Trifle 37

Oatmeal Raisin Cookie Trifle 38

Peaches N' Cream Trifle 39

Peanut Butter Cookie Trifle 40

Pineapple Strawberry Trifle 41

Pumpkin Tiramisu Trifle 42

Red Velvet With Cream Cheese Trifle 43

Strawberries N' Cream Trifle 44

Strawberry Banana Trifle 45

Strawberry Tiramisu Trifle 46

Summer Berry Trifle 47

Vanilla Trifle 48

White Chocolate Almond Trifle 49

Other Cookbooks By Dan Moyer 50

Notes From Family Of The Author

"If you're going to make just one trifle recipe from this cookbook, make it the Cookies & Cream Cheesecake Trifle. This was my family's favorite dessert in the whole book. My wife and three small children couldn't get enough of the flavor overload that this trifle brings to the table. No one will go to bed hungry when this dessert is served."

-Ryan Moyer, author's brother

"Strawberries and Cream Trifle

This trifle was the perfect end to a hot summer's day. The fresh strawberries and whipped cream complimented each other perfectly. My family and I truly enjoyed every bite of this sweet cool dessert. Thank you, Dan for allowing me to take an early taste test! This will be my go to dessert for all of our family's summer gatherings."

-Kelli Moyer, author's sister in law

"I have tried many of the trifles in this book, my favorites have to be Coffee Cake, Cherry Cheesecake, and Blueberry Pie. Each one of these has distinct flavors I was pleasantly surprised to taste. The Coffee Cake Trifle is made with chunks of streusel topping that remind me of eating an actual coffee cake. The Cherry Cheesecake Trifle tastes similar to eating a cheesecake, which is a favorite of mine. The Blueberry Pie Trifle is made with canned pie filling and fresh blueberries which gives the desert a fresh, summery feel. Overall, I have sampled many trifles and all are wonderful."

-Maria Simon, author's sister

"Over the last few weeks, my family and I have tried many of the recipes in this book, and have enjoyed them all! Each family member has their own personal favorite, and mine personally is the Coffee Cake Trifle, with the Cherry Cheesecake Trifle a close second. A trifle is one of the more visually appealing desserts that you can serve, and for as impressive as these look, the taste is even better. If you need to impress a crowd or that special someone, look no further than this book!"

-Rob Simon, author's brother in law

Introduction

Thank you for purchasing Amazing Trifle Recipes (previously titled "Delicious Trifle Recipes 2". This is the second installment in this series of trifle cookbooks by me, Dan Moyer. This book is for those who enjoy delicious, easy to make layered desserts. Whereas the first book in this series focused mostly on traditional dessert flavors, this book focuses heavily on both traditional and very creative dessert flavors. While trifles may appear elaborate, they are actually quite simple to make.

One day many years ago my brother in law's sister brought over a layered dessert in a fancy glass bowl. Blueberries, raspberries and lemon pudding stacked up nicely, and blended together for a delectable array of flavors. I asked what it was called, and from then on I became hooked on trifles.

Trifles are traditionally served in tall glass bowls. They consist of alternating layers of dessert items of different flavors and textures. Many of the recipes in this book are based off existing classic dessert flavors (Blueberry Pie, Coffee Cake, Coconut Cream Pie, etc.), as well as many very creative flavors (Strawberry Tiramisu, Cherry Vanilla, Maple Cheesecake, etc.) The recipes in this book are very simple to prepare, even for those with little experience cooking or baking. Few recipes involve the stovetop, and most require premade mixes and/or cans of pie filling from the baking aisle.

Trifle bowls can be purchased at many department stores, as well as on amazon.com. These recipes are designed for three and a half quart trifle bowls. This gives you fourteen servings at one cup each for every recipe.

If you have a larger or smaller bowl, you can try increasing or decreasing certain parts to the recipe. Let's say you have a one gallon trifle bowl and you're making the Chocolate Covered Strawberry Trifle. Instead of using two small boxes of chocolate pudding mix, you can use two of the larger boxes of pudding mix and use six cups of milk, as well as more strawberry halves. If you have a three quart bowl and are making the Oatmeal Raisin Cookie Trifle, you can buy one larger box of vanilla pudding mix instead of two small ones and use three cups of milk. You can also use less oatmeal raisin cookies. If you use a different amount of pudding than what is called for and it calls to add something to it, like an extract, cinnamon, peanut butter, etc., make sure you adjust those ingredients and the milk to keep the correct proportions. Depending on the size of your bowl, increasing or decreasing whipped topping is always an option. And if your bowl is larger, you can always follow the recipe as is and just not to fill it up the whole way.

These recipes can be converted for individual parfaits by lessening the amounts of the layers. If making parfaits and the recipe calls for brownies or cake, you can buy individual size brownies or slices of cake from a store, restaurant, bakery, etc. This will save you from making an entire cake or pan of brownies, most of which you may not use.

Certain items in every Ingredients list are meant to be "reserved for garnish" and are optional. They are not required until the very end to decorate, if you choose to do so, and are not included in the Instructions or Layering sections.

When you need to make pudding with extracts added in, make sure you pay close attention to the correct amount of milk called for in the Ingredients list and not what the box calls for. If you add the amount of milk the box calls for and the extract, the pudding will become too runny.

Each recipe calls for certain amounts of whipped topping. Buy the kind of whipped topping you would scoop out of a container, not the kind that sprays out of a can.

If a recipe calls for cake, I recommend patting down the layers of cake pieces a little bit after you put them in the bowl. This will conserve space in the bowl and leave more room for the other layers.

If layers appear uneven, don't worry about it. It's hard to make a trifle look perfect and will taste delicious regardless.

Whether your favorite is the Chocolate Rum Cake Trifle, Pumpkin Tiramisu Trifle, Cinnamon Donut Trifle, or you just can't decide, you'll have 42 recipes that will be a hit with your family and friends!

Banana Cream Pie Trifle

Banana cream, what a dream

Ingredients:
*1 box (about 12 oz.) vanilla wafers
*½ cup (1 stick) melted butter
*2 boxes (3.4 oz. each) banana cream instant pudding mix
*4 cups whole milk
*2 medium bananas
*1 medium banana, reserved for garnish (optional)
*2 cups orange juice (for soaking banana chunks)
*4 ½ cups whipped topping

Instructions:
1. In large bowl, crumble the vanilla wafers. Then add melted butter and gently mix. If desired, reserve ½ cup of the mixture for garnish.
2. In separate large bowl, combine banana cream pudding mixes and milk. Mix for 2 minutes, let sit for 5 minutes.
3. Peel banana and slice into several small chunks. Pour orange juice into a 12 oz. or larger glass. Soak the chunks in the orange juice for 5 minutes. If desired, do the same with the reserved banana so it can be used for garnish. (This process is to delay browning.) Set banana chunks aside.

Layering: (Does not include items reserved for garnish)
(From bottom to top of 3 ½ quart trifle bowl)
Half the vanilla wafer mixture
Half the banana cream pudding
Half the banana chunks
Half the whipped topping
Repeat layers once in same order.

Garnish: (Optional)
See Instructions. Sprinkle reserved vanilla wafer mixture over top trifle. Then arrange reserved banana chunks on top any way you want.

(Note: Soaking the banana chunks in orange juice will only delay browning. It is recommended that this trifle be eaten the same day it is made.)

Blackberry Crisp Trifle

Berry sweet, berry good

Ingredients:
*3 cups flour
*1 ¾ cups brown sugar
*3 cups quick oats
*2 teaspoons ground cinnamon
*2 cups (4 sticks) melted butter
*3 cans (21 oz. each) blackberry pie filling
*4 cups whipped topping

Instructions:
1. In large bowl, combine flour, brown sugar, quick oats, ground cinnamon and melted butter. Mix together. After crisp topping has cooled, break apart into bite size pieces. If desired, reserve 6-10 pieces of the crisp topping for garnish.
2. If desired, reserve ½ cup blackberry pie filling for garnish.

Layering: (Does not include items reserved for garnish)
(From bottom to top of 3 ½ quart trifle bowl)
A quarter of the crisp topping pieces
Half the blackberry pie filling
A quarter of the crisp topping pieces
Half the whipped topping
Repeat layers once in same order.

Garnish: (Optional)
See Instructions. Spoon reserved blackberry pie filling into center on top. Then place reserved crisp topping pieces in a circle around the pie filling.

Blueberry Pie Trifle

You won't feel blue with this trifle

Ingredients:
*2 sleeves graham crackers
*1 cup (2 sticks) melted butter
*2 teaspoons sugar
*3 cans (21 oz. each) blueberry pie filling
*3 cups blueberries, washed
*8 blueberries, washed, reserved
for garnish (optional)
*1 ½ teaspoons lemon juice
*4 cups whipped topping
*¾ cup whipped topping, reserved for
garnish (optional)

Instructions:
1. Crumble graham crackers in large bowl.
Then add melted butter and sugar. Gently mix.
2. In separate large bowl, combine blueberry
pie filling, blueberries and lemon juice. Gently mix. If desired, reserve ¼ cup pie filling for
garnish.

Layering: (Does not include items reserved for garnish)
(From bottom to top of 3 ½ quart trifle bowl)
Half the graham cracker mixture
Half the blueberry pie filling
Half the whipped topping
Repeat layers once in same order.

Garnish: (Optional)
See Instructions. Spoon reserved blueberry pie filling into center on top. Using a frosting piping
bag and any tip, make 8 small mounds with the reserved whipped topping going around the
inside rim of the bowl. Then place one reserved blueberry on top of each mound.

Brownie Ice Cream Sundae Trifle

Enjoy any day, not just on Sundae

Ingredients:
*1 box brownie mix, plus ingredients called
for in package instructions
*2 boxes (3.4 oz. each) vanilla instant pudding mix
*3 cups whole milk
*1 cup vanilla ice cream
*chocolate syrup
*chocolate syrup, reserved for garnish (optional)
*rainbow sprinkles
*rainbow sprinkles, reserved for garnish (optional)
*5 ½ cups whipped topping
*1 tablespoon whipped topping, reserved for
garnish (optional)
*1 maraschino cherry, reserved for garnish
(optional)

Instructions:
1. Set vanilla ice cream in refrigerator for several hours or overnight to melt (melting at room temperature is not recommended). Then, in a large bowl, combine vanilla pudding mixes, milk and melted vanilla ice cream. Mix for two minutes, let sit for 5 minutes.
2. Prepare brownies according to package instructions. If desired, after cooling reserve a single serving brownie square to be used for garnish. Then break apart the rest of the brownies into bite size pieces.

Layering: (Does not include items reserved for garnish)
(From bottom to top of 3 ½ quart trifle bowl)
Half the brownie pieces
Half the vanilla pudding/ice cream mixture
A drizzling of chocolate syrup
A sprinkling of rainbow sprinkles
Half the whipped topping
Repeat layers once in same order.

Garnish: (Optional)
Drizzle reserved chocolate syrup over top trifle in any design you want. Then sprinkle reserved rainbow sprinkles over top. Place reserved brownie square in the center on top and then put reserved whipped topping on top of the brownie. If necessary, remove stem from reserved maraschino cherry and blot with a napkin. Place cherry on top of reserved whipped topping.

Butterscotch Toffee Bar Trifle

For the finer things in life

Ingredients:
*1 box brownie mix, plus ingredients called for in package instructions
*2 boxes (3.4 oz. each) butterscotch instant pudding mix
*4 cups whole milk
*1 package (about 10 oz.) miniature chocolate covered toffee bars
*5 cups whipped topping

Instructions:
1. Prepare brownies according to package instructions. After cooling, break apart into bite size pieces.
2. In large bowl combine butterscotch pudding mixes and milk. Mix for 2 minutes, let sit for 5 minutes.
3. Place 2 thirds of the miniature chocolate covered toffee bars in a blender (if you can't fit them all at once, do half at a time). Mix until they have all turned into fine crumbs. If desired, do the same with the other 1 third of the toffee bars to create a surplus for garnish. If doing so, set the extra toffee bar crumbs to the side and reserve them for garnish.

Layering: (Does not include items reserved for garnish)
(From bottom to top of 3 ½ quart trifle bowl)
Half the brownie pieces
Half the butterscotch pudding
Half the toffee bar crumbs
Half the whipped topping
Repeat layers once in same order.

Garnish: (Optional)
See Instructions. Sprinkle reserved toffee bar crumbs over top trifle.

Cherry Cheesecake Trifle

Very cherry

Ingredients:
*2 sleeves graham crackers
*½ graham cracker, reserved for garnish (optional)
*1 cup (2 sticks) melted butter
*2 teaspoons plus ½ cup sugar, *divided*
*6 oz. cream cheese
*1 ½ cups heavy whipping cream
*2 cans (21 oz. each) cherry pie filling
*1 teaspoon almond extract
*3 cups whipped topping
*about 10-15 maraschino cherries, reserved for garnish (optional)

Instructions:
1. Crumble the graham crackers in large bowl. Add melted butter and 2 teaspoons sugar. Gently mix together.
2. In separate large bowl, combine the ½ cup sugar, heavy whipping cream and cream cheese. Mix with electric mixer until thick and fluffy (may take several minutes).
3. In another separate large bowl, combine cherry pie filling and almond extract. Gently mix, trying not to break the cherries.

Layering: (Does not include items reserved for garnish)
(From bottom to top of 3 ½ quart trifle bowl)
Half the graham cracker mixture
Half the cream cheese mixture
Half the cherry pie filling
Half the whipped topping
Repeat layers once in same order.

Garnish: (Optional)
Finely crush reserved ½ graham cracker and sprinkle crumbs over top trifle. Remove stems from reserved maraschino cherries if necessary and blot cherries with napkin. Then arrange them any way you want over top of the trifle.

Cherry Lemon Trifle

A summertime treat

Ingredients:
*1 box lemon cake mix, plus ingredients called for in package instructions
*2 cans (21 oz. each) cherry pie filling
*1 teaspoon almond extract
*4 cups whipped topping
*about 8 maraschino cherries, reserved for garnish (optional)

Instructions:
1. Prepare lemon cake according to package instructions. After cooling, break apart into bite size pieces.
2. In large bowl, combine cherry pie filling and almond extract. Gently mix together, trying not to break the cherries. If desired, reserve ¼ cup pie filling for garnish.

Layering: (Does not include items reserved for garnish)
(From bottom to top of 3 ½ quart trifle bowl)
A quarter of the lemon cake pieces
Half the cherry pie filling
A quarter of the lemon cake pieces
Half the whipped topping
Repeat layers once in same order.

Garnish: (Optional)
See Instructions. Put reserved cherry pie filling in center on top. Remove stems from reserved maraschino cherries if necessary. Blot cherries with napkin and then arrange them around the inside edges on top, making a circle.

Cherry Vanilla Trifle

Cherry and vanilla, a delicious combination of flavors

Ingredients:

*1 box yellow cake mix, plus ingredients called for in package instructions
*2 cans (21 oz. each) cherry pie filling
*1 teaspoon almond extract
*1 box (5.1 oz.) vanilla instant pudding mix
*3 cups whole milk
*3 ½ cups whipped topping

Instructions:

1. Prepare yellow cake according to package instructions. After cooling, break apart into bite size pieces. If desired, reserve 4-6 tablespoons of yellow cake pieces for garnish.

2. In large bowl, combine vanilla pudding mix and milk. Mix for 2 minutes, let sit for 5 minutes.

3. In separate large bowl, combine cherry pie filling and almond extract. Gently mix, trying not to break the cherries. If desired, reserve 3-4 tablespoons of pie glaze for garnish.

Layering: (Does not include items reserved for garnish)
(From bottom to top of 3 ½ quart trifle bowl)
Half the yellow cake pieces
Half the cherry pie filling
Half the vanilla pudding
Half the whipped topping
Repeat layers once in same order.

Garnish: (Optional)
See Instructions. Spoon reserved pie glaze into center on top. Then sprinkle reserved yellow cake pieces in a circle around the pie glaze.

Chocolate Chip Cookie Dough Trifle

Rolling in the dough

Ingredients:
*1 box cookie brownie mix, plus ingredients called for in package instructions
*2 boxes (3.4 oz. each) vanilla instant pudding mix
*4 cups whole milk
*1 ½ lbs. edible chocolate chip cookie dough
*5 cups whipped topping

Instructions:
1. Prepare cookie brownies according to package instructions. After cooling, break apart into bite size pieces.
2. In large bowl, combine vanilla pudding mixes and milk. Mix for 2 minutes, let sit for 5 minutes.
3. Break apart cookie dough into bite size pieces. If desired, reserve 6-10 pieces of cookie dough to be used for garnish.

Layering: (Does not include items reserved for garnish)
(From bottom to top of 3 ½ quart trifle bowl)
Half the cookie brownie pieces
Half the vanilla pudding
Half the cookie dough pieces
Half the whipped topping
Repeat layers once in same order.

Garnish: (Optional)
See Instructions. Place one reserved cookie dough piece in the center on top, and then place the others in a circle going around the inside rim on top.

Chocolate Covered Strawberry Trifle

Fine and elegant

Ingredients:
*1 box chocolate cake mix, plus ingredients called for in package instructions
*2 boxes (3.4 oz. each) chocolate instant pudding mix
*4 cups whole milk
*3 cups strawberry halves, stems removed, washed
*5 whole strawberries, washed, reserved for garnish (optional)
*3 cups whipped topping
*1 bag (about 12 oz.) milk chocolate chips, reserved for garnish (optional)

Instructions:
1. Prepare chocolate cake according to package instructions. After cooling, break apart into bite size pieces.
2. In large bowl, combine chocolate pudding mixes and milk. Mix for 2 minutes, let sit for 5 minutes.

Layering: (Does not include items reserved for garnish)
(From bottom to top of 3 ½ quart trifle bowl)
A quarter of the chocolate cake pieces
A quarter of the chocolate pudding
Half the strawberry halves
A quarter of the chocolate pudding
A quarter of the chocolate cake pieces
Half the whipped topping
Repeat layers once in same order.

Garnish: (Optional)
Tear off a 1 foot strip of wax paper and set aside. Pour reserved chocolate chips into a small, microwavable bowl and microwave on high for 30 seconds. Remove from microwave and stir until it becomes a smooth mixture. Dip a reserved whole strawberry into chocolate mixture so that most of it (not the stem) is covered in chocolate. Remove from chocolate mixture and place on wax paper. Repeat this process with the 4 remaining whole strawberries, dipping each one, one at a time, into the mixture and placing them on the wax paper. Once the chocolate on the strawberries has hardened, place them on top of the trifle, with 1 in the middle and the other 4 around the inside edges, making the points of a square.

Chocolate Lovers' Trifle

So chocolatey

Ingredients:
*1 box chocolate cake mix, plus ingredients called for in package instructions
*2 boxes (3.4 oz. each) chocolate instant pudding mix
*4 cups whole milk
*2 ¼ cups milk chocolate chips
*1 cup milk chocolate chips, reserved for garnish (optional)
*1 tablespoon plus 1 ½ teaspoons corn syrup
*2 ¼ teaspoons corn syrup, reserved for garnish (optional)
*⅔ cup heavy whipping cream
*⅓ cup heavy whipping cream, reserved for garnish (optional)
*8 tablespoons chocolate frosting
*4 tablespoons chocolate frosting, reserved for garnish (optional)
*2 tablespoons plus 2 teaspoons chocolate syrup
*1 tablespoon plus 1 teaspoon chocolate syrup, reserved for garnish (optional)
*3 cups whipped topping

Instructions:
1. Prepare chocolate cake according to package instructions. After cooling, break apart into bite size pieces.
2. Combine chocolate pudding mixes and milk in large bowl. Mix for 2 minutes, let sit for 5 minutes.
3. In medium sauce pan over medium heat, combine milk chocolate chips, corn syrup, and heavy whipping cream. (If desired, add in reserved milk chocolate chips, reserved corn syrup, and reserved heavy whipping cream to make a surplus to be used for garnish.) Stir constantly until completely melted. Remove from heat, then add in chocolate frosting and chocolate syrup. Stir until thoroughly mixed. (If making a surplus for garnish, mix in reserved chocolate frosting and reserved chocolate syrup, and then reserve 1 third of mixture for garnish.) Let mixture cool to the point that it is thick but still easy to spread, then immediately start the Layering process. (Note: The chocolate mixture should be made after the cake and pudding.)

(Continued next page)

Chocolate Lovers' Trifle

(Continued)

Layering: (Does not include items reserved for garnish)
(From bottom to top of 3 ½ quart trifle bowl)
A quarter of the chocolate cake pieces
Half the chocolate pudding
A quarter of the chocolate cake pieces
Half the chocolate mixture
Half the whipped topping
Repeat layers once in same order.

Garnish: (Optional)
See Instructions. Spread reserved chocolate mixture over top of trifle. If desired, let some spread over the rim and down sides of bowl. (You should put paper towels underneath the trifle bowl if you want the chocolate mixture to run down sides of bowl. Chocolate mixture will become more solid when it cools completely.)

Chocolate Malt Ball Trifle

This trifle really packs a whopper

Ingredients:
*1 box brownie mix, plus ingredients called
for in package instructions
*1 box (3.4 oz.) vanilla instant pudding mix
*1 box (3.4 oz.) chocolate instant pudding mix
*4 cups whole milk
*2 boxes (5 oz. each) chocolate covered malt
balls
*5 cups whipped topping

Instructions:

1. Prepare brownies according to package
instructions. After cooling, break apart into bite
size pieces.
2. In large bowl, combine vanilla pudding mix,
chocolate pudding mix, and milk. Mix for 2
minutes, let sit for 5 minutes.
3. If desired, reserve 20-25 individual chocolate covered malt balls for garnish.

Layering: (Does not include items reserved for garnish)
(From bottom to top of 3 ½ quart trifle bowl)
Half the brownie pieces
Half the vanilla/chocolate pudding
Half the chocolate covered malt balls
Half the whipped topping
Repeat layers once in same order.

Garnish: (Optional)
Place reserved chocolate covered malt balls on top of trifle.

Chocolate Rum Cake Trifle

Yo cocoa and a bottle of rum!

Ingredients:
*1 box chocolate cake mix
(do not follow package instructions)
*½ cup water
*½ cup (1 stick) melted butter
*4 eggs
*3 boxes (3.4 oz. each) chocolate instant
pudding mix
*¾ cup chopped pecans
*½ cup gold rum
*4 cups whole milk
*4 cups whipped topping
*1 cocktail umbrella for garnish (optional)

Instructions:
1. Preheat oven to 325 degrees. Grease a
9" by 13" cake pan (a traditional Bundt
pan is not necessary, as you will be breaking the chocolate rum cake into bite size pieces). Set
pan aside. In large bowl, combine chocolate cake mix, water, melted butter, eggs, 1 box
chocolate pudding mix, pecans, and gold rum. Mix together. Pour batter into pan and bake in
oven. After about 26 minutes, check to see if it is fully baked by inserting a knife into center. If
the knife comes out clean, the cake is fully baked. If not, continue checking like this every few
minutes. After cooling, break apart into bite size pieces. If desired, reserve 5-10 tablespoons of
chocolate rum cake pieces for garnish.
2. In separate large bowl, combine 2 boxes of chocolate pudding mix and milk. Mix for 2
minutes, let sit for 5 minutes.

Layering: (Does not include items reserved for garnish)
(From bottom to top of 3 ½ quart trifle bowl)
A quarter of the chocolate rum cake pieces
Half the chocolate pudding
A quarter of the chocolate rum cake pieces
Half the whipped topping
Repeat layers once in same order.

Garnish: (Optional)
See Instructions. Sprinkle reserved chocolate rum cake pieces over top trifle. Then insert cocktail
umbrella on an edge on top

Cinnamon Apple Cheesecake Trifle

Fall into this rich autumn dessert

Ingredients:
*2 sleeves cinnamon graham crackers
*½ cinnamon graham cracker, reserved for garnish (optional)
*1 cup (2 sticks) melted butter
*2 teaspoons plus ½ cup sugar, *divided*
*6 oz. cream cheese
*1 ½ cups heavy whipping cream
*2 teaspoons ground cinnamon
*¾ teaspoon ground cinnamon, reserved for garnish (optional)
*2 cans (21 oz. each) apple pie filling
*3 cups whipped topping

Instructions:
1. Crumble cinnamon graham crackers in large bowl. Add melted butter and 2 teaspoons sugar. Gently mix.
2. In separate large bowl combine ½ cup sugar, heavy whipping cream, cream cheese and ground cinnamon. Mix with electric mixer until thick and fluffy (may take several minutes).

Layering: (Does not include items reserved for garnish)
(From bottom to top of 3 ½ quart trifle bowl)
All the cinnamon graham cracker mixture
All the cinnamon cream cheese mixture
All the apple pie filling
All the whipped topping

Garnish: (Optional)
Sprinkle reserved ground cinnamon over top trifle. Then finely crush reserved half cinnamon graham cracker and sprinkle crumbs over top.

Cinnamon Donut Trifle

A great dessert to start your day

Ingredients:
*30-35 cinnamon powdered mini ring donuts
*6 cinnamon powdered mini ring donuts, reserved for garnish (optional)
*2 boxes (3.4 oz. each) vanilla instant pudding mix
*4 cups whole milk
*½ teaspoon ground cinnamon
*5 cups whipped topping

Instructions:
1. Cut each cinnamon powdered mini ring donut in half.
2. In large bowl, combine vanilla pudding mixes and milk. Mix for 2 minutes, let sit for 5 minutes. Then add ground cinnamon and mix.

Layering: (Does not include items reserved for garnish)
(From bottom to top of 3 ½ quart trifle bowl)
A quarter of the mini donut pieces
Half the cinnamon/vanilla pudding
A quarter of the mini donut pieces
Half the whipped topping
Repeat layers once in same order.

Garnish: (Optional)
Make a cut into 1 reserved mini ring donut and hang on the rim of the bowl, like a lemon slice. Then place the remaining 5 reserved mini ring donuts on top of the trifle.

CMP Trifle

Chocolate, marshmallow and peanuts, a delicious combination

Ingredients:
*1 box brownie mix, plus ingredients called for in package instructions
*2 boxes (3.4 oz. each) white chocolate instant pudding mix
*4 cups whole milk
*1 cup marshmallow cream
*1 cup peanuts, unsalted
*½-1 cup peanuts, reserved for garnish (optional)
*chocolate syrup
*chocolate syrup, reserved for garnish (optional)
*4 ½ cups whipped topping
*1 cup mini marshmallows, reserved for garnish (optional)

Instructions:
1. Prepare brownies according to package instructions. After cooling, break apart into bite size pieces.
2. In large bowl, combine white chocolate pudding mixes and milk. Mix for 2 minutes, then let sit for 5 minutes. Then add marshmallow cream and mix thoroughly.

Layering: (Does not include items reserved for garnish)
(From bottom to top of 3 ½ quart trifle bowl)
Half the brownie pieces
Half the marshmallow pudding
Half the peanuts
A drizzling of chocolate syrup (over top peanuts)
Half the whipped topping
Repeat layers once in same order.

Garnish: (Optional)
Place reserved mini marshmallows in center on top. Then sprinkle reserved peanuts around the marshmallows. Drizzle reserved chocolate syrup over top peanuts.

(Note: This trifle must be kept covered when not being served or the mini marshmallows on top will go stale.)

Coconut Cream Pie Trifle

An exotic delight

Ingredients:

*2 sleeves graham crackers
*1 cup (2 sticks) melted butter
*2 teaspoons sugar
*2 boxes (3.4 oz. each) coconut cream instant pudding mix
*4 cups whole milk
*2 cups sweetened coconut flakes
*1 cup sweetened coconut flakes, reserved for garnish (optional)
*5 cups whipped topping

Instructions:

1. Crumble graham crackers in large bowl. Then add melted butter and sugar. Gently mix.
2. In separate large bowl, combine coconut cream pudding mixes and milk. Mix for 2 minutes, let sit for 5 minutes.
3. Preheat oven to 350 degrees. Place sweetened coconut flakes on a baking sheet (if desired, add in reserved coconut flakes to make a surplus for garnish). Bake for about 5 minutes (during the baking process you should carefully remove the pan from the oven a few times and stir the flakes. Do this carefully.) Several of the flakes should be golden brown. After cooling, if you added in the reserved coconut flakes set them aside to be used for garnish.

Layering: (Does not include items reserved for garnish)
(From bottom to top of 3 ½ quart trifle bowl)
Half the graham cracker mixture
Half the coconut cream pudding
Half the toasted coconut flakes
Half the whipped topping
Repeat layers once in same order.

Garnish: (Optional)
See Instructions. Sprinkle reserved toasted coconut flakes over top trifle.

Coffee Cake Trifle

Enjoy with a cup of Joe

Ingredients:

*1 box coffee cake mix or crumb cake mix, plus ingredients called for in package instructions
*1 box (3.4 oz.) vanilla instant pudding mix
*1 box (3.4 oz.) butterscotch instant pudding mix
*4 cups whole milk
*1 teaspoon plus 2 ½ teaspoons ground cinnamon, *divided*
*1 ½ teaspoons ground cinnamon, reserved for garnish (optional)
*⅔ cup flour
*⅓ cup flour, reserved for garnish (optional)
*1 ½ cup sugar
*¾ cup sugar, reserved for garnish (optional)
*¾ cup (1 ½ sticks) melted butter
*¼ cup (½ stick) melted butter, reserved for garnish (optional)
*3 ½ cups whipped topping

Instructions:

1. Prepare coffee cake or crumb cake according to package instructions. After cooling, break apart into bite size pieces.
2. In large bowl, combine vanilla pudding mix, butterscotch pudding mix and milk. Mix for 2 minutes, let sit for 5 minutes. Then add 1 teaspoon ground cinnamon and mix.
3. For the streusel topping, in separate large bowl combine flour, sugar, melted butter and 2 ½ teaspoons ground cinnamon. Mix with a whisk until mixture is solid and lumpy. (It will be a smooth liquid at first but keep mixing.) If desired, add in reserved flour, reserved sugar, reserved melted butter and reserved ground cinnamon to this process to create a surplus to be used for garnish. If creating a surplus for garnish, reserve 1 third of streusel topping for the end.

Layering: (Does not include items reserved for garnish)
(From bottom to top of 3 ½ quart trifle bowl)
Half the coffee cake or crumb cake pieces
Half the vanilla/butterscotch/cinnamon pudding mixture
Half the streusel topping
Half the whipped topping
Repeat layers once in same order.

Garnish: (Optional)
See Instructions. Sprinkle reserved streusel topping over trifle.

Cookies N' Cream Cheesecake Trifle

Who put cheesecake in the cookie jar?

Ingredients:
*2 packages (about 15 oz. each) chocolate sandwich cookies
*½ cup (1 stick) melted butter
*6 oz. cream cheese
*½ cup sugar
*1 ½ cups heavy whipping cream
*5 ½ cups whipped topping

Instructions:

1. If desired, reserve 1 whole chocolate sandwich cookie for garnish. Then put the rest of the cookies into a blender and mix until most of them are fine crumbs. (If your blender is not big enough to fit all of them at once, try doing portions of them at a time.) Transfer crumbs to a large bowl and then crumble any cookies that did not get blended. (Do not crumble cookies with your hands while they are still in the blender.) Remove 2 cups of cookie crumbs from the bowl and reserve them for Step 2. Then add melted butter to the remaining cookie crumbs and mix.

2. In separate large bowl, combine cream cheese, sugar, and heavy whipping cream. Mix with electric mixer until thick and fluffy (may take several minutes). Then add the 2 cups of cookie crumbs that you reserved in Step 1. Mix.

Layering: (Does not include items reserved for garnish)
(From bottom to top of 3 ½ quart trifle bowl)
Half the cookie crumb/butter mixture
Half the cream cheese/cookie crumb mixture
Half the whipped topping
Repeat layers once in same order.

Garnish: (Optional)
See Instructions. Remove filling from reserved chocolate sandwich cookie and crush the sides into fine crumbs. Sprinkle crumbs over top trifle.

English Trifle With Sherry

The traditional trifle

Ingredients:

*1 box pound cake mix, plus ingredients called for in package instructions
*½ cup sherry
*2 cups strawberry jam
*2 boxes (3.4 oz. each) lemon instant pudding mix
*4 cups whole milk
*1 cup blueberries, washed
*a few extra blueberries, washed, reserved for garnish (optional)
*1 cup strawberry halves, stems removed, washed
*a few extra strawberry halves, stems removed, washed, reserved for garnish (optional)
*1 cup raspberries, washed
*a few extra raspberries, washed, reserved for garnish (optional)
*3 cups whipped topping
*1-2 cups whipped topping, reserved for garnish (optional)

Instructions:

1. Preheat oven to 350 degrees. Grease a 9" by 13" cake pan and set aside. Prepare batter for pound cake according to package directions. Pour batter into pan and bake. After about 17 minutes, check to see if it is fully baked by sticking a knife into the center. If it comes out clean, it is fully baked. If not, keep checking like this every few minutes. When the pound cake is done baking, remove from the oven and let cool. After cooling, cut 2 thirds of the cake into squares, about 2 inches each. (The other 1 third of the cake will not be used in the trifle, so you may do what you want with it.)
2. In large bowl, combine lemon pudding mixes and milk. Mix for 2 minutes, let sit for 5 minutes.

(Continued next page)

English Trifle With Sherry

Layering: (Does not include items reserved for garnish)
(From bottom to top of 3 ½ quart trifle bowl)
Half the squares of pound cake
Half the sherry (pour evenly over the pound cake squares, sherry will soak into them)
Half the strawberry jam
Half the lemon pudding
Half the blueberries, half the strawberry halves, and half the raspberries (all on one layer)
Half the whipped topping
Repeat layers once in same order.

Garnish: (Optional)
Using a frosting piping bag and any tip, make several small mounds with the reserved whipped topping on top of the trifle. Place one reserved blueberry, reserved strawberry half, or reserved raspberry on top of each mound.

Fudge Trifle

Smooth and rich

Ingredients:
*1 box fudge brownie mix, plus ingredients called for in package instructions
*2 boxes (3.4 oz. each) chocolate fudge instant pudding mix
*4 cups whole milk
*1 pound chocolate fudge
*5 cups whipped topping

Instructions:
1. Prepare fudge brownies according to package instructions. After cooling, break apart into bite size pieces.
2. In large bowl, combine chocolate fudge pudding mixes and milk. Mix for 2 minutes, let sit for 5 minutes.
3. Cut chocolate fudge into bite size squares. If desired, reserve 4 squares of fudge for garnish.

Layering: (Does not include items reserved for garnish)
(From bottom to top of 3 ½ quart trifle bowl)
Half the fudge brownie pieces
Half the chocolate fudge pudding
Half the chocolate fudge squares
Half the whipped topping
Repeat layers once in same order.

Garnish: (Optional)
See Instructions. Place reserved chocolate fudge squares on top of trifle near the inside rim, making the points of a square.

Key Lime Pie Trifle

Time for key lime

Ingredients:
*2 sleeves graham crackers
*1 graham cracker, reserved for garnish (optional)
*2 teaspoons sugar
*1 cup (2 sticks) melted butter
*2 boxes (3.4 oz. each) vanilla instant pudding mix
*3 ¾ cups whole milk
*1 teaspoon lime extract
*12-14 drops neon green food coloring (optional)
*5 cups whipped topping
*1 lime slice, reserved for garnish (optional)

Instructions:
1. Crumble graham crackers in large bowl. Add sugar and melted butter. Gently mix.
2. In separate large bowl combine vanilla pudding mixes and milk. Mix for 2 minutes, then let sit for 5 minutes. Then add lime extract and, if desired, neon green food coloring. Mix thoroughly.

Layering: (Does not include items reserved for garnish)
(From bottom to top of 3 ½ quart trifle bowl)
Half the graham cracker mixture
Half the key lime pudding
Half the whipped topping
Repeat layers once in same order.

Garnish: (Optional)
Finely crush reserved graham cracker into fine crumbs and sprinkle them over top trifle. Then make a cut halfway into reserved lime slice and hang it on the rim of the bowl.

(Note: A recipe for a Key Lime Pie Trifle appeared in earlier editions of the first trifle cookbook in this series. It has since been removed and replaced with a recipe for a different trifle. The recipe on this page is different than the Key Lime Pie Trifle recipe that appeared in the first book.)

Lemon Blueberry Trifle

A springtime dessert

Ingredients:
*1 box lemon cake mix, plus ingredients called for in package instructions
*2 boxes (3.4 oz. each) lemon instant pudding mix
*4 cups whole milk
*2 cups blueberries, washed
*½ cup blueberries, washed, reserved for garnish (optional)
*4 ½ cups whipped topping
*1 lemon slice, reserved for garnish (optional)

Instructions:
1. Prepare lemon cake according to package instructions. After cooling, break apart into bite size pieces.
2. In large bowl, combine lemon pudding mixes and milk. Mix for 2 minutes, let sit for 5 minutes.

Layering: (Does not include items reserved for garnish)
(From bottom to top of 3 ½ quart trifle bowl)
Half the lemon cake pieces
Half the lemon pudding
Half the blueberries
Half the whipped topping
Repeat layers once in same order.

Garnish: (Optional)
Sprinkle reserved blueberries over top trifle. Make a cut halfway into reserved lemon slice and hang on rim of bowl.

Macadamia Nut Cookie Trifle

One smart cookie

Ingredients:
*2 packages macadamia nut cookie mix
(each package should make about 15 servings), plus
ingredients called for in package instructions
*2 tablespoons melted butter
*2 boxes (3.4 oz. each) white chocolate instant
pudding mix
*4 cups whole milk
*5 ½ cups whipped topping

Instructions:

1. Prepare macadamia nut cookies according to
package instructions. After all cookies have cooled,
take about 2 thirds of the cookies and put them in a
blender. Mix thoroughly until the cookies have turned
into fine crumbs. (If you can't fit all of them into your
blender at once, do portions of them at a time.)
Transfer crumbs to a large bowl. Add melted butter and gently mix. If desired, reserve 5
tablespoons of cookie crumb mixture for garnish.

2. Take remaining cookies and break each into a few smaller pieces. If desired, keep 4 cookies
whole and reserve them for garnish.

3. In separate large bowl, combine white chocolate pudding mixes and milk. Mix for 2 minutes,
let sit for 5 minutes.

Layering: (Does not include items reserved for garnish)
(From bottom to top of 3 ½ quart trifle bowl)
Half the macadamia nut cookie crumb/butter mixture
Half the white chocolate pudding
Half the macadamia nut cookie pieces
Half the whipped topping
Repeat layers once in same order.

Garnish: (Optional)
See Instructions. Sprinkle reserved cookie crumb/butter mixture over top trifle. Take reserved
whole macadamia nut cookies and stick them sideways into the top layer of whipped topping,
sticking them in just enough so they stand upright.

Maple Cheesecake Trifle

Sweet and creamy

Ingredients:
*2 sleeves graham crackers
*1 whole graham cracker, reserved for garnish (optional)
*1 cup (2 sticks) melted butter
*2 teaspoons plus ½ cup sugar, *divided*
*6 oz. cream cheese
*1 ½ cups heavy whipping cream
*1 teaspoon maple extract
*1 ½ teaspoons pure maple syrup
*2 tablespoons pure maple syrup, reserved for garnish (optional)
*5 cups whipped topping

Instructions:
1. Crumble the graham crackers in large bowl. Then add melted butter and 2 teaspoons sugar. Gently mix.
2. In separate large bowl, combine cream cheese, ½ cup sugar, and heavy whipping cream. Mix with electric mixer until thick and fluffy (may take several minutes). Then add maple extract and pure maple syrup. Mix.

Layering: (Does not include items reserved for garnish)
(From bottom to top of 3 ½ quart trifle bowl)
Half the graham cracker mixture
Half the maple cream cheese mixture
Half the whipped topping
Repeat layers once in same order.

Garnish: (Optional)
Finely crush reserved graham cracker and sprinkle crumbs over top trifle. Then drizzle reserved pure maple syrup over top.

Maple Pecan Trifle

Sweet and nutty

Ingredients:

*1 box yellow cake mix, plus ingredients called for in package instructions
*2 boxes (3.4 oz. each) vanilla instant pudding mix
*3 ¾ cups whole milk
*1 teaspoon maple extract
*1 cup chopped pecans
*½ cup chopped pecans, reserved for garnish (optional)
*4 tablespoons pure maple syrup
*2 tablespoons pure maple syrup, reserved for garnish (optional)
*4 cups whipped topping

Instructions:

1. Prepare yellow cake according to package instructions. After cooling, break apart into bite size pieces.
2. In large bowl, combine vanilla pudding mixes and milk. Mix for 2 minutes, let sit for 5 minutes. Then add maple extract and mix.

Layering: (Does not include items reserved for garnish)

(From bottom to top of 3 ½ quart trifle bowl)
Half the yellow cake pieces
Half the maple pudding
Half the chopped pecans
Half the pure maple syrup (drizzle over top pecans)
Half the whipped topping
Repeat layers once in same order.

Garnish: (Optional)

Sprinkle reserved chopped pecans over top trifle. Then drizzle reserved pure maple syrup over top pecans.

Maple Pumpkin Trifle

An autumn treat

Ingredients:

*1 box pumpkin bread mix, plus ingredients called for in package instructions
*8 tablespoons pure maple syrup
*2 tablespoons pure maple syrup, reserved for garnish (optional)
*2 boxes (3.4 oz. each) vanilla instant pudding mix
*3 ¾ cups whole milk
*1 teaspoon maple extract
*5 cups whipped topping

Instructions:

1. Prepare pumpkin bread according to package instructions. After cooling, break apart into bite size pieces. If desired, reserve 3 tablespoons of pumpkin bread pieces for garnish.
2. In large bowl, combine vanilla pudding mixes and milk. Mix for 2 minutes, let sit for 5 minutes. Then add maple extract and mix.

Layering: (Does not include items reserved for garnish)

(From bottom to top of 3 ½ quart trifle bowl)
A quarter of the pumpkin bread pieces
A quarter of the maple syrup (drizzle over top pumpkin bread pieces)
Half the maple pudding
A quarter of the pumpkin bread pieces
A quarter of the maple syrup
Half the whipped topping
Repeat layers once in same order.

Garnish: (Optional)

See Instructions. Sprinkle reserved pumpkin bread pieces over top trifle. Then drizzle reserved maple syrup over top trifle.

Marshmallow Trifle

Yummy and marshmallowy

Ingredients:
*1 box white cake mix, plus ingredients called for in package instructions
*2 boxes (3.4 oz. each) white chocolate instant pudding mix
*4 cups whole milk
*1 cup marshmallow cream
*2 cups mini marshmallows
*1 cup mini marshmallows, reserved for garnish (optional)
*3 ½ cups whipped topping

Instructions:
1. Prepare white cake according to package instructions. After cooling, break apart into bite size pieces.
2. In large bowl, combine the white chocolate pudding mixes and milk. Mix for 2 minutes, let sit for 5 minutes. Then add marshmallow cream and mix thoroughly.

Layering: (Does not include items reserved for garnish)
(From bottom to top of 3 ½ quart trifle bowl)
Half the white cake pieces
Half the marshmallow pudding
Half the mini marshmallows
Half the whipped topping
Repeat layers once in same order.

Garnish: (Optional)
Sprinkle reserved mini marshmallows over top trifle.

(Note: This trifle needs to be kept covered when not being served or the mini marshmallows on top will go stale.)

Mint Chocolate Chip Cheesecake Trifle

Mint is where the money's at

Ingredients:
*1 box brownie mix, plus ingredients called for in package instructions
*6 oz. cream cheese
*½ cup sugar
*1 ½ cups heavy whipping cream
*1 teaspoon mint extract
*9-10 drops green food coloring (optional)
*1 cup mini chocolate chips
*¼ cup mini chocolate chips, reserved for garnish (optional)
*5 ½ cups whipped topping

Instructions:
1. Prepare brownies according to package instructions. After cooling, break apart into bite size pieces.
2. In large bowl, combine cream cheese, sugar, heavy whipping cream, mint extract and, if desired, green food coloring. Mix with electric mixer until thick and fluffy (may take several minutes).

Layering: (Does not include items reserved for garnish)
(From bottom to top of 3 ½ quart trifle bowl)
Half the brownie pieces
Half the mint cream cheese mixture
Half the mini chocolate chips
Half the whipped topping
Repeat layers once in same order.

Garnish: (Optional)
Sprinkle reserved mini chocolate chips over top trifle.

Mocha Walnut

Sometimes you feel like a nut

Ingredients:
*1 box brownie mix, plus ingredients called for in package instructions
*2 boxes (3.4 oz. each) chocolate instant pudding mix
*3 cups whole milk
*1 cup black coffee, chilled
*1 cup walnut chips
*½ cup walnut chips, reserved for garnish (optional)
*5 cups whipped topping

Instructions:
1. Prepare brownies according to package instructions. After cooling, break apart into bite size pieces.
2. In large bowl, combine chocolate pudding mixes, milk and coffee. Mix for 2 minutes, let sit for 5 minutes.

Layering: (Does not include items reserved for garnish)
(From bottom to top of 3 ½ quart trifle bowl)
Half the brownie pieces
Half the chocolate/mocha pudding
Half the walnut chips
Half the whipped topping
Repeat layers once in same order.

Garnish: (Optional)
Sprinkle reserved walnut chips over top trifle.

Oatmeal Raisin Cookie Trifle

A classic cookie

Ingredients:
*2 packages oatmeal cookie mix (each should make about 15-18 servings) plus ingredients called for in package instructions
*½ cup raisins
*2 tablespoons melted butter
*2 boxes (3.4 oz. each) vanilla instant pudding mix
*4 cups whole milk
*5 cups whipped topping

Instructions:
1. Preheat oven according to package instructions of the oatmeal cookie mixes. In large bowl, combine both packages of oatmeal cookie mix, the ingredients called for on both packages, and the raisins. Mix. Then bake cookies according to package instructions. After cooling, set ¼ of the cookies aside. They are not needed in this trifle and you may do what you want with them. Take ⅔ of the remaining cookies and crumble them in a separate large bowl. Add melted butter and mix.
2. If desired, reserve 4 of the other ⅓ cookies and reserve them for garnish (keep them whole). Break the rest of the cookies apart, each into a few pieces.
3. In another separate large bowl, combine vanilla pudding mixes and milk. Mix for 2 minutes, let sit for 5 minutes.

Layering: (Does not include items reserved for garnish)
(From bottom to top of 3 ½ quart trifle bowl)
Half the oatmeal raisin cookie crumb/butter mixture
Half the vanilla pudding
Half the broken oatmeal raisin cookie pieces
Half the whipped topping
Repeat layers once in same order.

Garnish: (Optional)
See Instructions. Insert reserved whole oatmeal raisin cookies sideways into the top of the trifle, sticking them in just enough so they stand upright.

Peaches N' Cream Trifle

Just peachy

Ingredients:
*1 box yellow cake mix, plus ingredients called for in package instructions
*2 cans (15 oz. each) sliced peaches
*2 boxes (3.4 oz. each) vanilla instant pudding mix
*4 cups whole milk
*4 cups whipped topping, *divided*

Instructions:
1. Prepare yellow cake according to package instructions. After cooling, break apart into bite size pieces.
2. In large bowl, combine vanilla pudding mixes and milk. Mix for two minutes, let sit for 5 minutes. Then add 1 cup whipped topping and mix thoroughly.
3. Drain the cans of peach slices. If desired, reserve a few peach slices for garnish.

Layering: (Does not include items reserved for garnish)
(From bottom to top of 3 ½ quart trifle bowl)
Half the yellow cake pieces
Half the sliced peaches
Half the vanilla pudding mixture
1 ½ cups whipped topping
Repeat layers once in same order.

Garnish: (Optional)
See Instructions. Place reserved peach slices in center on top.

Peanut Butter Cookie Trifle

Peanut buttery

Ingredients:

*1 box peanut butter cookie brownie mix, plus
ingredients called for in package instructions
*2 boxes (3.4 oz. each) vanilla instant
pudding mix
*4 cups whole milk
*⅔ cup creamy peanut butter
*1 package peanut butter cookie mix (should make
about 15-18 servings), plus ingredients called for in
package instructions
*4 cups whipped topping

Instructions:

1. Prepare peanut butter cookie brownies according
to package instructions. After cooling, break apart
into bite size pieces.
2. In large bowl, combine vanilla pudding mixes
and milk. Mix for 2 minutes, let sit for 5 minutes.
Then add peanut butter and mix thoroughly.
3. Prepare peanut butter cookies according to package instructions. After cooling, break cookies
apart, each into a few pieces. If desired, keep 4 cookies whole and reserve them for garnish.

Layering: (Does not include items reserved for garnish)
(From bottom to top of 3 ½ quart trifle bowl)
Half the peanut butter cookie brownie pieces
Half the peanut butter pudding
Half the peanut butter cookie pieces
Half the whipped topping
Repeat layers once in same order.

Garnish: (Optional)
See Instructions. Insert reserved whole peanut butter cookies sideways into trifle, sticking them
into the top layer just enough so that they stand up.

Pineapple Strawberry Trifle

A tropical treat

Ingredients:

*1 box pineapple cake mix, plus ingredients called for in package instructions
*2 cans (21 oz. each) strawberry pie filling
*2 cans (20 oz. each) pineapple chunks or crushed pineapple (see Step 3 of Instructions)
*4 cups whipped topping
*3 pineapple rings from a can, reserved for garnish (optional)
*3 very small strawberries, washed, reserved for garnish (optional)

Instructions:

1. Prepare pineapple cake according to package instructions. After cooling, break apart into bite size pieces.
2. If desired, reserve 3-4 tablespoons of strawberry pie filling glaze for garnish.
3. When deciding whether to use pineapple chunks or crushed pineapple, consider which texture of pineapple you would prefer within the trifle. Drain the pineapple chunks or crushed pineapple.

Layering: (Does not include items reserved for garnish)

(From bottom to top of 3 ½ quart trifle bowl)
Half the pineapple cake pieces
Half the strawberry pie filling
Half the pineapple chunks or crushed pineapple
Half the whipped topping
Repeat layers once in same order.

Garnish: (Optional)

Place reserved pineapple rings on top of trifle. Cut off stems of reserved strawberries and place one, cut side down, inside each pineapple ring. (You may have to cut off more of the strawberries to make them fit.) See Instructions. Spoon reserved strawberry pie glaze in between the pineapple rings.

Pumpkin Tiramisu Trifle

A new dessert for Thanksgiving

Ingredients:
*about 50 soft lady fingers (each about 3 inches long, 1 inch wide, ½ inch high)
* ¾ cup black coffee, chilled
*1 box (3.4 oz.) butterscotch instant pudding mix
*2 cups whole milk
*1 ½ cups pumpkin pie mix (do not buy "pure pumpkin")
*1 tablespoon plus 2 teaspoons ground cinnamon, *divided*
*1 teaspoon ground cinnamon, reserved for garnish (optional)
*1 container (8 oz.) mascarpone cheese
*4 ½ cups whipped topping

Instructions:
1. Using a spoon, drizzle coffee evenly over lady fingers. (Do not dip lady fingers into the coffee.)
2. In large bowl, combine butterscotch pudding mix and milk. Mix for 2 minutes, let sit for 5 minutes. Then add pumpkin pie mix, 1 tablespoon ground cinnamon, and mascarpone cheese. Mix thoroughly.

Layering: (Does not include items reserved for garnish)
(From bottom to top of 3 ½ quart trifle bowl)
A quarter of the lady fingers
Half the pumpkin pudding mixture
1 teaspoon ground cinnamon (sprinkle evenly)
A quarter of the lady fingers
Half the whipped topping
Repeat layers once in same order.

Garnish: (Optional)
Sprinkle reserved ground cinnamon evenly over top trifle.

Red Velvet With Cream Cheese Trifle

A shade of red and a burst of flavor

Ingredients:
*1 box red velvet cake mix, plus ingredients called for in package instructions
*6 oz. cream cheese
*½ cup sugar
*1 ½ cups heavy whipping cream
*3 ½ cups whipped topping

Instructions:
1. Prepare red velvet cake according to package instructions. After cooling, break apart into bite size pieces. If desired, reserve 5-8 tablespoons of red velvet cake pieces for garnish.
2. In large bowl combine cream cheese, sugar, and heavy whipping cream. Mix with electric mixer until thick and fluffy (may take several minutes).

Layering: (Does not include items reserved for garnish)
(From bottom to top of 3 ½ quart trifle bowl)
A quarter of the red velvet cake pieces
Half the cream cheese filling
A quarter of the red velvet cake pieces
Half the whipped topping
Repeat layers once in same order.

Garnish: (Optional)
See Instructions. Sprinkle reserved red velvet cake pieces over top trifle.

Strawberries N' Cream Trifle

A creamy delight

Ingredients:
*1 box white cake mix, plus ingredients
called for in package instructions
*2 boxes (3.4 oz. each) vanilla instant
pudding mix
*4 cups whole milk
*5 cups whipped topping, *divided*
*3 cups strawberry halves, stems removed, washed
*1 whole strawberry, washed, reserved
for garnish (optional)

Instructions:
1. Prepare white cake according to package
instructions. After cooling, break apart into bite size
pieces.
2. In large bowl combine vanilla pudding mixes and
milk. Mix for 2 minutes, let sit for 5 minutes. Then
add 1 cup whipped topping and mix thoroughly.

Layering: (Does not include items reserved for garnish)
(From bottom to top of 3 ½ quart trifle bowl)
Half the white cake pieces
Half the vanilla pudding mixture
Half the strawberry halves
2 cups whipped topping
Repeat layers once in same order.

Garnish: (Optional)
Place reserved whole strawberry on top of trifle in the center.

Strawberry Banana Trifle

Two great flavors in one trifle

Ingredients:

*1 yellow cake mix, plus ingredients called for
in package instructions
*2 boxes (3.4 oz. each) banana cream instant
pudding mix
*4 cups whole milk
*3 cups strawberry halves,
stems removed, washed
*8 strawberry halves, stems removed,
washed, reserved for garnish (optional)
*4 cups whipped topping

Instructions:

1. Prepare yellow cake according to package
instructions. After cooling, break apart into bite
size pieces. If desired, reserve 5-8 tablespoons
of yellow cake pieces for garnish.
2. In large bowl, combine banana cream
pudding mixes and milk. Mix for two minutes, then let sit for 5 minutes.

Layering: (Does not include items reserved for garnish)

(From bottom to top of 3 ½ quart trifle bowl)
Half the yellow cake pieces
Half the banana cream pudding
Half the strawberry halves
Half the whipped topping
Repeat layers once in same order.

Garnish: (Optional)

See Instructions. Sprinkle reserved yellow cake pieces over top trifle. Then arrange reserved
strawberry halves on top any way you want.

Strawberry Tiramisu Trifle

A delicacy

Ingredients:
*about 50 soft lady fingers (each about
3 inches long, 1 inch wide, ½ inch high)
*1 box (5.1 oz.) vanilla instant pudding mix
*3 cups strawberry milk
*1 package (7.5 oz.) strawberry cream
cheese
*5 cups whipped topping
*1 whole strawberry, washed, reserved for
garnish (optional)

Instructions:
1. In large bowl, combine vanilla pudding
mix and strawberry milk. Mix for 2 minutes,
let sit for 5 minutes. Then add strawberry
cream cheese and mix thoroughly.
2. If desired, reserve 4 individual lady fingers
to be used for garnish.

Layering: (Does not include items reserved for garnish)
(From bottom to top of 3 ½ quart trifle bowl)
A quarter of the lady fingers
Half the strawberry pudding
A quarter of the lady fingers
Half the whipped topping
Repeat layers once in same order.

Garnish: (Optional)
See Instructions. Make a square on top of the trifle in the center using the reserved lady fingers.
Place reserved whole strawberry in the middle.

Summer Berry Trifle

A light summer delight

Ingredients:
*1 box angel food cake mix, plus ingredients
called for in package instructions
*4 cups strawberry yogurt
*1 cup strawberry halves,
stems removed, washed
*6 strawberry halves, stems removed, washed,
reserved for garnish (optional)
*1 cup raspberries, washed
*6 raspberries, washed, reserved for
garnish (optional)
*1 cup blueberries, washed
*6 blueberries, washed, reserved for
garnish (optional)
*4 cups light whipped topping

Instructions:
1. Prepare angel food cake according to package
instructions. After cooling, break apart into bite size pieces.

Layering: (Does not include items reserved for garnish)
(From bottom to top of 3 ½ quart trifle bowl)
Half the angel food cake pieces
Half the strawberry yogurt
Half the strawberry halves, half the raspberries and half the blueberries (all on one layer)
Half the light whipped topping
Repeat layers once in same order.

Garnish: (Optional)
Arrange reserved strawberry halves, reserved raspberries, and reserved blueberries on top of
trifle any way you want.

Vanilla Trifle

Who said vanilla was boring?

Ingredients:
*1 box vanilla cake mix, plus ingredients called for in package instructions
*2 boxes (3.4 oz. each) vanilla instant pudding mix
*3 ¾ cups whole milk
*¾ teaspoon vanilla extract
*4 ½ cups whipped topping

Instructions:
1. Prepare vanilla cake according to package instructions. After cooling, break apart into bite size pieces. If desired, reserve 5-6 tablespoons of vanilla cake pieces for garnish.
2. In large bowl, combine vanilla pudding mixes and milk. Mix for 2 minutes, let sit for 5 minutes. Then add vanilla extract and mix.

Layering: (Does not include items reserved for garnish)
(From bottom to top of 3 ½ quart trifle bowl)
A quarter of the vanilla cake pieces
Half the vanilla pudding
A quarter of the vanilla cake pieces
Half the whipped topping
Repeat layers once in same order.

Garnish: (Optional)
See Instructions. Sprinkle reserved vanilla cake pieces over top trifle.

White Chocolate Almond Trifle

A white delight

Ingredients:
*2 sleeves graham crackers
*2 teaspoons sugar
*1 cup (2 sticks) melted butter
*2 boxes (3.4 oz. each) white chocolate instant pudding mix
*4 cups whole milk
*1 cup almonds
*½ cup almonds, reserved for garnish (optional)
*4 ½ cups whipped topping

Instructions:
1. Crumble graham crackers in large bowl. Add sugar and melted butter. Gently mix.
2. In separate large bowl combine white chocolate pudding mixes and milk. Mix for 2 minutes, let sit for 5 minutes.

Layering: (Does not include items reserved for garnish)
(From bottom to top of 3 ½ quart trifle bowl)
Half the graham cracker mixture
Half the white chocolate pudding
Half the almonds
Half the whipped topping
Repeat layers once in same order.

Garnish: (Optional)
Sprinkle reserved almonds overtop trifle.

Other Cookbooks On Amazon By Dan Moyer:

Delicious Trifle Recipes: 42 Easy To Make Layered Desserts (First book in this series)

Delicious Milkshake Recipes: 40 Easy To Make Shakes

Printed in Great Britain
by Amazon